A LITANY ON LOSS

TAWIAH NAANA AKUA MENSAH

For you
For never stopping
Even when it hurts . . .

* * *

Published by Akashic Books
©2023 Tawiah Naana Akua Mensah
ISBN: 978-1-63614-127-5

Akashic Books
Brooklyn, New York
Instagram, Twitter, Facebook:
@AkashicBooks
E-mail: info@akashicbooks.com
Website: www.akashicbooks.com

African Poetry Book Fund
Prairie Schooner
University of Nebraska
110 Andrews Hall
Lincoln, Nebraska 68588

TABLE OF CONTENTS

PREFACE

by Matthew Shenoda

In this contemplative gathering of poems, Tawiah Naana Akua Mensah pulls the reader into a world heavy with quiet consideration and begins an exploration of what it means to navigate a coming-of-age as a woman in Ghana. Driven by the experiential, *A Litany on Loss* seeks to ask questions rather than answer them, attempting to parse how one might regard the familial and intimate relationships in their lives in that moment between being and becoming.

In poems that work to untangle the innate connections of mother and daughter and to define the intergenerational struggles with misogyny and identity, *A Litany on Loss* presents a narrative arc that tells plainly what it means for Mensah to come into a sense of self forever connected to, but differing from, her mother. In her attempt to understand the antecedents of their relationship, she writes:

> Look at me, Mother. Do you see me
> or do you only see him?
> Am I beautiful? Or will I always look like pain?

> ("Unwanted. Unplanned. Undead.")

It is moments like these in which Mensah identifies the fullness of her mother and her mother's own struggles as a woman as Mensah comes into her own as a daughter that make these poems resonant and impactful. Regarding the advice passed down to her through a lineage of women, women who have been disparaged and left to settle for less, Mensah recalls her mother's words:

My mother tells me to find a love that comes home
no matter how long it stays gone and keep it.
That sometimes love comes home smelling of wine,
tasting of other women,
and all things outside.
That this fragile thing is a burden to bear
and it's mine alone.

("Who Would Love a Storm Like Me?")

For Mensah, as for many of her generation, she cannot
fully embrace the counsel of her mother, nor can she accept the
position of subservience, having seen its effects and how it has
damaged the generation of women before her. Mensah responds:

But I've never been good at holding fragile things.
Whether it is a set of fine china,
or your brother's ailing heart.
I am a raging storm on most days
and my anger feels like a house on fire.
Only, this house is mine.

("Who Would Love a Storm Like Me?")

In poem after poem, Tawiah Mensah works to decipher how
one comes into themselves in the lineages of tradition and trauma,
how to hold the anger and hurt, and what the line might be be-
tween the realities we have made for ourselves and what might
be beyond our tangible understanding. Mensah contemplates
the ways so many, often those most discarded by society and

certain traditions, embody a sense of divinity as a way of understanding the struggles of the world:

> On some days god is different things.
> A single mother.
> A newborn with a terminal disease.
> A barren woman's first labor.

> ("On Some Days, God.")

As these poems continue to reveal themselves, we see Mensah's arrival into her rightful place in society as she further defines the understandings she has garnered about herself. She writes with sharp lucidity:

> But when you welcome the weather into your home,
> You should always be ready for a storm.

> ("I'm Too Much of a Breathing Fire to Be a Convenient Option.")

A heeding and a warning, an acceptance and moment of pride, *A Litany on Loss* quietly details the author's own becoming. This chapbook is a welcome and iterative sense of discovery that, while deeply personal, is resonant across myriad generations and cultures. These poems begin to help us understand, through a specific lens, the age old "litany of losses" where one generation loses a bit of the previous in an effort to propel us all into a future that can respect and recognize the struggles of the past and attempt, in part, not to repeat them.

UNWANTED. UNPLANNED. UNDEAD.

Forgive me Mother for I have caused you to sin. That I carry the face of
your hurt to mock you.

Look at me, Mother. Do you see me
or do you only see him?
Am I beautiful? Or will I always look like pain?

Do I remind you of the man
who took your soul and wore your body
till you had nowhere to hide within yourself?
Am I always going to be your pain?
Am I always going to be my father's child?

If I had to pull and peel till all traces of him would disappear,
I'd start from the eyes,
the same ones that carried all the anger.

It would not matter the parts of me that had to die with
him.
I would not rest, till you held me with a body that shook
with want.

FAMILIAR.

I lay awake and listen to the tremble in the earth, the weary in the wind
My eyes marry into the darkness,
and all of them come alive
My father's angry eyes, my mother's despair,
my brother's silence.
Everything comes alive,
breathing and beating the life out of me

The part of me that recognizes the ruin
as the only home it's ever known,
stretches to reel it in and begs till I'm consumed into oneness.
A sameness with the tremor.

When you ask me where I go in my sleep,
What it looks like over there,
What do I become?
What are these things I say in my sleep?

I want to tell you that I go home,
—the walls look nothing like my house,
the one you often visit.
I want to tell you that I am trapped and surrounded
in the very place I left them buried.
Even in my sleep, I still run.

And one of these days,
when you see my lips part
and I begin to speak of things you have never heard
When I start to speak in a language so foreign to you,

Maybe hold me, wait for me, pray for me.
Beg God, until I find my way home to you.

WHO WOULD LOVE A STORM LIKE ME?

My mother tells me to find a love that comes home
no matter how long it stays gone and keep it.
That sometimes love comes home smelling of wine,
tasting of other women,
and all things outside.
That this fragile thing is a burden to bear
and it's mine alone.

But I've never been good at holding fragile things.
Whether it is a set of fine china,
or your brother's ailing heart.
I am a raging storm on most days
and my anger feels like a house on fire.
Only, this house is mine.

It is a constant battle of me trying to rescue the softness of my past,
giving life to the parts of me that knew how to be a soft tender woman.
The bloodbath is like an abattoir,
when I stretch into my body
and let in the light,
the hearty laughs,
the eager eyes,
so this body knows what it means to be loved right.

When I speak of love
it must be a meteor falling at once.
A Jericho, tumbling down,
Or a love that leaves you bleeding like an open battlefield.

TIME OF DEATH: 6:23 P.M.

Like a corpse
I lay motionless and emptied of all that makes me whole and good.
Of all who hold my saneness in place.
There are no books on how to unlearn everything you know about a person.
From the curve of their smile to the story
behind the scar above their right eye.

The worst days are when death decides to choose us so we become a shell
of what we used to know.
How do you go on living when a part of you dies?
When is it okay to let go? How long is long enough?
There are good days, like when we have won, carried our beds, our faith
and continued to live.
And there is the chaos of a loss that leaves in stages,
tearing apart piece by piece along its dreadful path.
We choose to no longer cry each day.
Instead, we wait until grief returns,
pouring in a rush.

ON SOME DAYS, GOD.

On different days I have died
in a room full of people
and a home with no windows.

On other days I have lived
in a little space of heaven
and a place in between.

Life has a way of teaching you things
or grabbing you by your hair
throwing you face-first in a fight.
It puts a song in your heart and dares you to dance.

Death makes you appreciate the courtesy of the sun in the early morning;
"I will come . . . I will sit with you every wake. So shall it be."
Loss stays till you beg for the silence of the night.
You could scream and only the wind would embrace you.

On some days god is different things.
A single mother.
A newborn with a terminal disease.
A barren woman's first labor.

THE ONLY WAY I KNOW TO LIVE.

To write my truth
means to draw in the night
and watch as vultures feed
on my open heart till I come pouring in a storm.

But I can also be calm-waters,
a hopeless lover,
a broken friend,
and a daughter who never stays long enough to catch her mother fall.

I sit with my arms crossed as danger spills like rage.
I do not wear my scars, I become them,
live, breathe, and speak them.

I come with a map that shows
where the half dead of my past are buried.
If you cut me open deep enough,
they come climbing out, gasping for air.

I lay awake and leave it to the monsters that pull
till I am drenched in my fears
and screaming out the story of each grave
and where they are buried.

MY MOTHER TAUGHT ME TO SPEAK SILENCE.

The first time I heard a war song was from my mother.
It didn't come melting like morning praise.
I heard it move with the beat of her heart.
Breaking the wall between her spine and her voice.
Even now, I see the chords escape violently when she breathes.

The second time I heard a war song was on April 25.
I cried for the chords to gather within me.
I welcomed them with my jaw apart,
yet all they did was swallow him whole.

Every night it rains,
I feel his digging,
I taste his breath,
I remember my body torn apart into maps.
And a man hunting for the miracles of life. "*Why didn't I scream?*"
Have you been listening?
My mother taught me to speak silence.

STORIES OF THE WOMEN BEFORE ME.

I was born fearless, by a fire-full woman.
I speak with the fear and bravery of my mother.
The first thing she fed me was her fight.
So, when I say no,
I'm speaking to all the times she wanted to say so, and could not.

I live with her blood beating in my chest.
Running to my spine to fight for what should have been hers.
And Oh! When I love, I love like a wave and fire.
Taking it all. Whole and at once.
Because her blood in my veins will have it no other way.

TEACHING MY MOTHER TO LIVE.

I asked her what it was about him that made her tremble with want?
Who was this man that left her aching with a softness?
She said:

He reaches for my body like every part of me holds a promise he cannot wait to devour.

I screamed:
Now, why would anyone think this magic is not worth shielding?
This soul-snatching, body-consuming, star-exploding piece of magic?

Oh, darling,
great men have failed.
If mirrors could speak
they would shatter every time you walked,
starting with a scream.
It would be a disaster for a broken man to carry all this magic.

In all the places to find healing and yours is in the dwelling of the broken.

THERE IS NOTHING HOLY ABOUT A STORM.

There is nothing holy about a storm.
It awakens in the absence of a father.
Rages at the uncle whose hands went a little too far too deep.
Then it comes alive in a lover that takes and takes
but never finds roots deep enough to stay.

There is nothing holy about cutting yourself open
for a man to bury his sadness and leave it within you.
When there is no more joy to feed.
When there is nowhere else to fill.
Where do you go with a void that heavy?

There is nothing holy about pouring the language of fear
into the mouth of your daughter.
Telling her to swallow and never push it out.
A home is a home
because she can clench her teeth and bite her tongue.
Even when it's swollen black and blue.
Even when it weighs with the taste of other women.
Even then. Especially then.

PRAYERS OF A DEAD MAN.

I've heard people say that they know.
As the clock nears the end,
they hear it tick. tick and tock
So why didn't he hold my mother
like a soul clinging to its savior?
Why didn't he ask
If there were any wonders I'd like to see?

The day before he died,
I listened to his heartbeat as he slept.
It was slow, careful, and weighing with all the stories he never told.
A history we never knew existed.
I had questions that stuck on my tongue, eager for answers,
but were too afraid to crawl out of my mouth.

The day before he died it was pouring outside.
I saw him look out the window.
I heard him whisper to the midnight wind.
Telling her to carry his love to our home, like a song.
To remind my mother that she was the greatest journey of his life.
To find his daughter a love that restores.
To bring peace to the son,
who would learn that anger does not stay long enough
to mask the guilt of absence.

TILL YOU CALL US BY NAME.

I was born with a color that sits with the sun,
And tells stories about cracked clay pots and fighting women.
I was born with arrows drawn on my face,
showing men with claws where to dig in and feast.

My people live with freedom nailed in their feet.
When the night comes, the moon calls us by name.
And we rise, carve our hearts on boards,
and leave fear behind closed doors.

Even when the only way to stay alive
is to swallow our teeth.
Still, we fight. Still, we chant.
Holding hands with our feet taped to the ground.
And with all the weapons we carry.
A hashtag, a Twitter thread, a flag, a voice.
The mist may sting our eyes and burn our nostrils,
metal may rip through our flesh, and our skin may scald.

We do not back down.
We do not stay back.
Our fight is all we have.
This fire is who we are.
Our freedom is all we know.

I'M TOO MUCH OF A BREATHING FIRE TO BE A CONVENIENT OPTION.

As much as I'd like to hide it,
There are parts of me that love the sadness.
The breaking. The shattering. The undoing of myself.
There are parts of me that dwell in it.
They choose to sit under the stars and coin stories of a boy I've never met,
choose the girl in the little red dress,
and leave me behind at the cinema.

I've been told I'm too hopeful.
I free a grudge before the next sun goes down.
I leave the door open for people who refuse to stay.
I wait for them to walk back in
and sing me my praise of gratitude.
As if to say I'm the price and how dare they wish to do better than me.
But when you welcome the weather into your home,
You should always be ready for a storm.

EVEN GOD WANTS NO PART OF THIS.

Over here, poems stay breathing on sheets and never make it out.
There are stories that stay hidden in our backs
because the mouth is a home of things unsaid.

Not a day goes by where I do not look at my body and sigh,
Thank you for knowing how to hide my scars.

A wound only heals when it's covered up.
So why does this itch have me digging and pulling out of myself to be whole?
Where do I go when the words become too heavy
yet I cannot find a home to curl into, be swallowed, and run away from the
    world?
What do I do when the very thing that saves me
threatens to drown me in the open?
Do I look like a thing God would want?
My heart is heavy with sadness,
and when I kneel the clouds come crashing before I part my lips to say *save*.
You say God likes to fix broken things,
but even I know I am past putting them together.
Nobody likes a tearful eye, beaten black and blue.

HOW TO BURY LOVE THAT DIES.

Allow yourself to touch the waves when they come for you.
Allow yourself to drown in them when they call out to you,
but never leave without your song;

And when you come back, washed up, crashed against the stones,
when they ask you where you have been,
who you saw,
and where they are, just tell them.

Sometimes we win,
sometimes we come apart like shattering glass
—gracefully and all at once—
Not all love stays, not all love wins.

YOU WOULD LOVE IT HERE, I PROMISE.

At 23 all the lovers have come and toured this city, tired.
There are no more holy temples to be worshipped.
Just remnants of a name I still speak, with a stutter.

I read a story once
about a girl who gathered her anger and her warmth,
set herself on fire,
and never let out a cry.
I envy her strength and thirst after her freedom.
The most I have ever done for my body
is to drown her in the fury of people
who never stay long enough to learn her last name.

AN OPEN CONFESSION.

The last person who lived here had to tiptoe his way through
because who would want to wake a darkness, strong enough to consume you?
You could scream but that only takes longer.
It's easier to sit, watch, and wait till it ravages you whole.
Where will you go with these scars that say you came, you saw
—and even though you died a little on the way, you lived.

When they ask about the mess, I say I have a hunger
for men who leave me a little broken and torn apart into maps.
When they leave I struggle to find my way home.
And as if the mourning makes it easier to bear a loss,
I fold and drown the sadness somewhere between my eyes,
the only testimony of all that has come and refused to stay,
and I wait for a new morning and a new prey.
This darkness will not be mine and mine alone.

LET ME SHOW YOU HOW I BECAME.

The first wrong things I learned about being a woman, I learned
from the women who carried me:
How to burn your body as an offering for a man.
How to swallow your tongue and quench your fight.
How to become a body of many women in one. For one.

The first right things I learned about being a woman,
I learned from the women who bathed me:
It does not matter how long it has been,
your wrath will find you and when it does.
You will remember the tremble in your belly
that shook till the the words came flooding every space within you.
You will wage war and win.
You will take back your own
and you will look him dead in the heart,
and say,
"I will not be reduced to a casualty of generational rage."

These women poured their sorrow into me,
fed me with it,
and taught me when to roar.

1 PETER 5:7 "CAST ALL YOUR ANXIETY ON HIM BECAUSE HE CARES FOR US."

Each time I go to God, I speak in whispers.
I lay it all down with a fright so heavy it weighs on my tongue.
I often chew on the big things.
—The vengeance that wrestles my heart, the guilt.
I bite them down in my mouth till they become less frightening.
I wouldn't want to scare Him off before He has a chance to save
me.
I hold my lips tightly together, beg them not to quiver.
I too want to be called saved.

It shouldn't be possible right?
To want to love a thing so much you consume its grief.
What in their right mind longs for broken things?
Everyone knows that love is the thing that wakes in the middle of the night,
and dares everything to fall to the ground.
How many more seasons, before you feed my grief back to me?

ACKNOWLEDGMENTS

"Till You Call Us by Name" and "Stories of the Women before Me" originally appeared in *A Voice Is a Voice: Resistance Issue.*